AuthorHouse™
1663 Liberty Drive
Bloomington, IN 47403
www.authorhouse.com
Phone: 1 (800) 839-8640

Published by AuthorHouse   11/18/2016

ISBN: 978-1-5246-5149-7 (sc)
ISBN: 978-1-5246-5147-3 (hc)
ISBN: 978-1-5246-5148-0 (e)

Library of Congress Control Number: 2016919490

Print information available on the last page.

Epiphany

Consciousness is the beginning, it just took the greater part of a lifetime to get to that point. The path to knowing yourself as yourself is the root of consciousness though most of us take it for granted. The subtlety that comes back to ruin us for this system and forces us to work to uncover a deeper understanding of everything. This started for me when I was seventeen, through the weight of teenage confusion and a childhood that I was happy to forget, a friend of the family decided to show some interest in me. I did not know it at the time but my education took off from that point as I was exposed to knowledge and experiences from men as much as fifteen to twenty-two years older than myself. We had conversations about music, culture, women, money and any topic that naturally arose. I was being prepared for life on my own but how could I repay these people for this unusual unexpected act of generosity and kindness. Some might even call it the highest form of love that we can muster, to see someone dead in the water and save him from himself.......

Transformation came in two phases. The first was very slow and entailed my emersion into the world of books. The first being a comic from Cuba called Groo, The Wanderer. It was not long until I moved on to rare books from the likes of Tuesday Lobsang Rampa, Chronicles of Tao by Den Ming Tao, Talks and Dialogs by Krishnamurty, Long walk to freedom by Nelson Mandela, Tao of Love and Sex and The Tao of Physics to name a few. The house was littered with books and the learning was not limited to the books I read but also the ones that he told me about that were recalled easily from a sharp memory. It was here that a black teenager in the Caribbean island of Trinidad gained a healthy respect for Hinduism and Buddhism. The teachings of Parmahansa Yogananda was a common topic and we were Rampa students so the customs of Tibet seemed natural to us. Actually spirituality became an all-inclusive search for truth and a healthy curiosity about eastern culture meant an appreciation of Chinese martial arts and ancient religions. I was definitely on my way to a life less ordinary as I soaked up these influences like a sponge.

For the next twenty two years I would try to live my life using the knowledge I gained during the three to five years after my mentor and friend came into my life. This was the slow first phase that I alluded to earlier. Through relationships, marriage, divorce and becoming a parent my experiences have always been strange. Common critiques would be that I think too much and always analyse everything. Apparently that's not good for socialising and fitting in. There was always a strong disconnect between how I saw things and the reality of others in the environment. What was it about life that makes things so difficult? Why can't we ever communicate in just the right way to get anything done? No one takes the time to listen, everyone is entitled to their own opinion and truth is for people who have time to waste. Everyone is spinning their own version of reality and in this mix you are advised to look out for number one.

Phase two came in April of 2015. After re-establishing contact with my mentor after a number of years being wrapped up in who I had become, he sent me an e-book that changed my life. Journey to the 9th Planet by Micheal Demarquet. I was so impressed by the information in this book that it inspired the final push to balance my education. The internet was now available to help with research areas that I was curious about. There I found Phill Valentine, Delbert Blair, Louis Farrakhan and many others. Suddenly the conspiracy theories were not out there anymore and no one was trying to discredit them anymore. The epiphany had arrived and after everything

I thought I knew, about a lot of things, most were not true. A lifetime of wondering why other people had such a poor handle on things led to me being the clueless one. Adrift in my mind lost in a sea of information, my mentor served as my only anchor. I had waited twenty two years for this breakthrough but he had spent about thirty-five to forty years searching for deeper insight into truth. Now we got to grow together in this new knowledge. A beginning for me that would provide the end of my education.

Consciousness is the beginning, to know yourself as yourself is a key to finding the mind behind the identity. To wear your identity like clothes and not be a slave to it. The beginning is to do what you have always done through the identity but not be afraid to go beyond that. Unlocking the mystery of how the brain creates an experience from electrical charges and knowing that everything we experience comes from perception. That ability of the brain to order events to ensure that we create what we need to experience. Consciousness is awareness, hypersensitivity, connectedness through reality to access the higher functioning of the mind. That was a mouthful but yes…..this is my epiphany.

How do we know ourselves? Drilling down to what are we but energy and thought, someone may ask why the two are separated. The TRUTH for us now in this time and space, is that we don't know what thought is. We have an idea what energy is in some of its forms but no idea what thought is. So we identify with our families, our bloodlines, our socialization and our culture. What if who we are shines through what we become and calls to us to act in accordance with our true nature despite the noise. The noise is all consuming with the advancements in technology. That is why we need to slow down and observe ourselves. It is natural for us to observe others but we do not observe our own thoughts, actions, reactions, intentions, traits, shortcomings and abilities. As my mentor would say, 'to deal with our situation we need to stop amalgamating our problems'.

Spirituality

Spirit beings in organic vessels. Keeping this point at the forefront of our mind is difficult because we seem to experience everything through the material world and the physical body. We are not socialised to remind ourselves about the emotion body and the power of thought. If we were focused on experiencing the world in its realest form then we would have to consider all the vibration states that interact in our environment. Unfortunately the psychology of behaviour has taken us in the opposite direction. The need to do less thinking and come to conclusions quickly has made it very difficult for most of us to change the way we do things. The ability to live a life guided by your spirit state is within everyone's grasp, but we do not know it. The limitation is always rooted in the societies we build and what we believe about the world.

The universe is never allowed to be a limitless source of possibility and we are taught that the brain is finite and its ability is limited. In fact this is how we trap the spirit in an organic prison.

Sharing my personal experiences with these matters help to ground some of the concepts as attainable for everyone. The earliest encounter of a different type of experience came after reading a few Lobsang Rampa books when I was about eighteen years old. He introduced the ideas about 'astral travel' and I understood that when we sleep our 'soul' would leave our body and go to the 'astral plain'. One night I was dreaming, which became common place for me, when I became aware that I was in a dream and I was observing myself but the rules of this place were different from when I was awake. I was on an ocean in a boat with no land in sight and no oars, there were no waves but the place was so peaceful. Just then a thought shot through my mind about fearing a killer whale attack, then instantly the surface of the water broke and time slowed down considerably. I could see the detail of the nose breaking the water and the richest black colour that I ever saw and the white of the belly. I experienced a mixture of fascination and paralysing fear. I fell out of the boat but the water was only ankle deep. Confusion, fear, heart racing and then I woke up. This was my very first conscious astral travel experience and it was quite a shock for the five senses and left my mind spinning with doubt and questions.

The next few years were spent doing one thing, conquering my fear in the astral. Here fear takes on a dimension of its own. It has levels and can actually push you out of the experience. Fear is an emotion and I did not know it then but it creates a vibration wave that speaks to the realest nature in matter. Fear paralyses you and stops you from using your imagination on the astral plain. Once handicapped you can't win. Free yourself in the astral and some of that confidence is experienced in your physical life. The unfortunate truth is that in ordinary life we are always afraid of something or the other. That you won't get that job, won't get that woman or man or won't be understood. This is actually ridiculous for beings with an immortal soul whose gift is to create with thought. To be a spirit being is to know that the universe was created for you to evolve as you create and exercise your free will. To embrace that this is your path through purpose, subjecting identity to be only a tool to gather experience. Every experience must be baked in circumstances and carry the meanings that you give it. The means can seem complicated but the goals are always simple. The only real learning is experiential knowledge.

Spirituality, morality and evolution are all words that are assigned specific meanings. We always try to marry them to the idea of being a good person and get lost in the rigid game that leaves no room for free will or dynamic expression. Beings of spiritual energy will inevitably evolve and universal law will have its way in determining what moral behaviour is. This can be the form but for most it is not. A person is a good person only until an event can cause them to be torn down and eventually there will be no good people and no one aspiring to be good. We have tried the congregations and fellowship and yet collective consciousness has not lead to heightened individual consciousness. The spiritual path is for the individual who must truly seek knowledge and the experiences will guide them.

The physical world that we live in relies on predictability and a confidence that comes from proving things. Science though was never meant to give a big picture view but rather to debunk parts of the story while giving proof for throwing it out. Matter gives the impression that there is animate and inanimate objects that make up our environment. However both sentient and inanimate objects are made of the same basic building blocks. The Atom is full of energy, some would say full of life and yet for our comfort, they can join together to be void of life or inanimate. Inanimate objects are seen as lacking consciousness because after all there is no irritability, movement, nutrition or reproduction as we observe them using our linear time and space. Matter is not solid. As human beings, we have never been able to get to the bottom of things, matter can always be subdivided. This view supports the view that it is not real, or rather it is only real to your five senses through your receptors. Vibration presents itself to be more real than matter as energy exists in waves of oscillation. Therefore we may be affected by waves of energy that we neither track nor care about and yet we claim that we are aware of our surroundings.

Life is characterised by the many ways that we separate our experience while on the planet. Race, sex, class, nationality, religion, education and family are all ways that we see the division in our world. What if none of these categories were real? Then the world would be very different indeed. What would we replace them with to create confusion and war? Make no mistake, war is necessary for us now because it is a consequence of our spiritual level at this point in time and space. We need separateness to create the 'them and us'. Our technological advancement has surpassed our spiritual development and like kids playing with matches we continue to light fires not caring about the consequences. The obvious answer then would be inclusion and interconnectedness right, but how do we get there. It is possible to stop separating ourselves from everything by paying attention to the choices we make and the information we draw upon to make those decisions. Question the things that you take for granted or rather that you think you are confident about. Thoughts are too important to have a base in shaky or abstract concepts. Everything that you have been taught as a child was not of your own doing, start there and re-educate yourself.

Case in point, we are told by the Tibetans and others that our bodies are made up of actually nine bodies. The three bodies that make up the Aura, the fluidic body, the emotion body, the mental body and dimensional aspects to our body. The tremendous complexity of the organic vessel is wasted on people who take it for granted. Whether through choice or ignorance the untapped potential for use of the body and mind costs us. Spirituality becomes a process where you use all the information available to order life to get the best out of the experience. Spirituality and science are not opposites. Science focuses on technology however the most sophisticated piece of technology is the organic machine that we identify as our body. What we know about ourselves should be used in everyday life to help with those nonstop decisions and thoughts. The facts that the body stores memory in the DNA, genes and the blood and the knowledge that the heart stores information as well as pumps blood may seem shocking but civilizations before us knew this. The knowledge passed down from pyramid writings, scrolls and time capsules show us the importance of blood lines and ancestry.

The individual trying to cultivate a way of being that resonate with his or her spirit state must consider what they put out and as a consequence what they attract. Love is the highest frequency of vibration and is the goal and tool of all spiritual being. To call something by a name is not the same as knowing it and the complexity within creation means that everything has levels of understanding, hence experiential knowledge. We are accustomed to low and medium frequency emotions in this time and space. If we are allowed to experience the blissful state of love it is only for a moment. Knowing this as a spiritually inclined student of life will help tremendously in your dealings with your family, in your marriages and in your friendships. You will discover that you can never really control another person but you can always try to control you interaction in the environment. Like I said before, slow things down, look at your thoughts and the origins of those thoughts and only launch them when you are satisfied that they will deliver what you want to create.

Perusing spiritual awareness and utilising consciousness in your identity or ego state is our goal however it is handicapped if we omit 'reincarnation'. The system of reincarnation is very sophisticated, allowing the consciousness to develop through all the levels of subtlety of creation. The thought based energy entity known as the consciousness gets to grow through its experiences both inside and outside of matter using all the variation that the physical world has to offer. Some would even argue that the experience of evolution goes beyond the physical

Universe in Creation. How can we know ourselves if we are not tested in matter? The physical world being the testing ground where rules govern down the celestial immortal being that does not know its true power. The knowledge of Reincarnation is very important because it allows us to work on specific tasks and know that we do not have to do everything or be everything in one lifetime. Divine planning takes on a new dimension because part of the plan is your idea to come down into matter to work on specific areas to advance your development. Spirit beings in organic vessels was our starting point and I trust that it takes on a deeper meaning after these shared consciousness points.

Soul Contract

What is the soul? I have referred to it here as consciousness. The part of the interplay in the physical world that is immortal in Creation. There are three points of reference that are involved in setting up an incarnation. The 'Over-soul', 'Astral body' and 'the identity body' are the three focus points. They are referred to by different names at times like, 'over-self', 'higher mind' and the 'ego' respectively. The over-self is actually a part of the spiritual system that marks a round of evolution for us. As we evolve by raising our vibration and the astral body moves to the next level over-self. This is done though, after the accumulation of experiences form many lives and while resolving the issues caused by past lives. In other words resolving your 'Karmic debt'. It has been said before that you raise your vibration by thinking higher level thoughts that resonate with higher frequency vibration. The astral body is you however you know yourself through an identity. This is why the ego must be created. It is not possible to know your astral body as yourself at this level. The design grounds you in the physical world through an identity and a physical body. The 'soul contract' is strictly for the ego.

The soul contract is extremely personal and depends on your level of experience, karmic debt, areas of focus, special projects started and attachments developed. When considering all these things an incarnation looks like a masterpiece of arrangements that we take for granted. It is built though to give us the best chance to get the flavour of experience that we need to grow spiritually. The soul contract may be the price of admission to the physical world but the environment provides challenges of its own. With over seven billion soul contracts running at the same time and each person having the ability to exercise free will, the school can get pretty complicated. The influences of others, the money system, socialization, religion, the education system, being cut off from your divine knowledge pool. It can all be very overwhelming. We end up making some mistakes over and over again until we work it out. The soul contract is likened to a rudder being used to navigate a sea of experiences to find your heading. Some people spend their whole lives talking about finding their purpose, their calling. Your purpose is to evolve and the soul contract tells you what to focus on now. The yogis tell us look within to find out what is real about ourselves.

If the soul contract was all that we were dealing with then life may still be simpler than it is. The stage of development of the astral body can attract roles in special projects in Creation. Purification through work. Also the over-self manages nine puppets at a time, sometimes more. The Creator presents itself through the complexity in Creation and it is difficult not to feel the weight of the grand design. The interconnectedness of the all is seen and experienced the deeper we probe into our experiences. So there are soul contracts, special roles and what my mentor likes to call 'add ons'. He describes these as tasks that should ideally be done by others but are passed to you because you are producing results. Yes, I know it's not fair and all that but it happens, and you do the work! Living an incarnation as though you are a spirit being in an organic vessel is work and that's why you came here.

In your search to discover your soul contract, be careful. Let things develop naturally. I have never tried to do conscious astral travel but rather I let the body sleep and then I have astral experiences. Development happens in its own way and should not be forced as you want to add on experience while doing no harm to yourself. Everything I have described thus far is quite natural and possible for every human being. The problem is that we do not like prolonged intense experiences. We need to take breaks to be a little silly then to come back to work when it pleases us. That will not work with this process, you must be honest with yourself, critical of your thoughts and take responsibility for your actions. Though work but you need you to do it. Our relationship with loved ones, animals, the environment and the planet depends on it. No, I am not a tree hugger or an atheist. I am a spirit being trying to raise my vibration and grow in the way the Creator's plan has laid out for me. I identify with my physical-ness only enough to unlock the subtlety in the experiences that I need.

The heightened awareness required to live like this comes from the development of the 'Pineal gland'. Some refer to it as our third eye, which helps us to go beyond the level of the senses. Heightened intuition leads to an experience where you attract the information that makes your journey possible. What you do with that information will dictate how fast and how far you develop. The experience is extremely personal though you may feel the need to share what is happening to you. Awakening from a state where you rationalise everything as being ok and workable can be difficult but you would not be seeing this new reality if it did not matter or did not play a role in your life. Remember you are not worked up and emotions are not flailing, this is a slow, calm realization that things are not as they seem in our environment. Trust yourself to recognise truth and follow your instincts. We are never alone, as conscious beings we are always connected with the energy in our environment.

The soul contract is part of a complex system that determines who we are. The storage of information in the body is fortunate as the soul contract can be married to our blood line to create particular flavours of experience. We are a point of convergence of four blood lines and we draw traits from all of them and pass it forward to our offspring. The world has lost sight of the importance of our ancestors however we continue to be affected by projects that they would have been involved in. Being a spirit being may mean that you will become aware of your ancestors and the ones you love can contact you in the dream state to communicate things that you need to know. Slowly you need to open your mind to greater possibilities and realities. Once again 'love' is seen as a powerful agent in our reality as spirits can create a bridge through a love connection with an ancestor. The reality that we were raised in presents so many mysteries and few answers as to how we should navigate this world, this heightened awareness is a gift and the application of it promises to be life changing.

2016

Months after the media blackout of the anniversary of the Million Man March in Washington, well into the war in Syria that expelled hundreds of thousands of refugees and an American Presidential campaign that threatens to release a mad man unto the world. 2016 is a different kind of year with energy in events all over the world. Five nations coming together to form BRIC and the financial world system going through massive shifts. After terrorist attacks in France and the UK voting to leave the European Union, media reports about new structures discovered in space and science spending considerable resources to figure out if our reality is a simulation. There is a general feeling of resolution of events started in 2015 that make you wonder, what's next. Time seems to be going by faster, consequences coming quicker and issues are not being allowed to settle. Locally in Trinidad and Tobago, the People's National Movement is in their first year of their term, our neighbour Venezuela is in crisis, our longest standing politician dies after forty four years of service. R.I.P. Mr. Manning. We continue to suffer from the oil price shocks that grip the world and our economy is in decline. The country becomes aware of the effects of gross corruption and mismanagement of resources in a time when revenue has contracted considerably.

The internet is now a part of our reality and is no longer a luxury item but a necessity. It provides multiple options for communication and technology develops so fast that people are required to learn new things on a constant basis to avoid the digital divide. Research can now be part of your daily routine and costs very little. The question has become, what are we going to do with this heightened state of awareness? How do we live in a global village? The events in America where 'Black Lives Matter' protects the extra judicial killing of a black man reaches me in real time. Waves of emotion sweep the world like never before in this new reality. Emotion, thought and your spirit state are at the centre of all events for you. For too long we have sent thoughts and emotions unchecked into our environment and we hope for peace, success in our business dealings or harmony where we live. The education we received through the years has a role in determining what we will be able to bounce back from. Trauma sometimes stop us from healing but this period of heightened awareness and questioning is an opportunity for all of us to work on raising our vibration. The power of the mind is not limited and the saviour that you are waiting for has already been gifted to you in your bloodline and your soul contract. The missing ingredient is the work for you to understand yourself. That is the mystery of looking within that the gurus tell you about. Introspection, patience, never putting yourself down, being fearless in your pursuits, seeking purity of your agendas and resisting the contamination of your pursuits by 'low vibration means'. We are here to get better at creating our reality.

Family life happens in two phases most times. There is the family that raised us and the family that we go on to create. Some of us have wonderful experiences growing up while others just want to forget. Early family life gives us our character disorders or our neuroses. There is a point where your family identity can become a prison, whether you had great experiences or horrible experiences. Let me remind you that the soul contract is aware of the conditions that you are coming to. However 'identifying' with a thing makes it real and your thoughts have power. So imagine that every opportunity that has ever come to you was based on how you perceive yourself, what you thought you deserved and what you were able to attract. Then there are the opportunities that we take advantage of and why. Choices, to exercise some kind of free will that causes our life to spin off tangentially to some new possibility. I know it is difficult at times to deal with family but if we let them only affect that early development but we take responsibility for what we create and step cautiously as we create our future, then we can do better. As my mentor says, 'he who knows better, must do better'.

Professionally I am a public servant, however I also consider myself a student of life. Possibly this is my grandest act of public service. Sharing an experience with you and exploring an individual path to discovering energy through really living. I lament the fact that people look at their careers too narrowly. What are you? You are part of a complex system of specialised jobs that serve the whole. Everything is interconnected. Yes, true but that's not how we operate. We go where the money is, either real money or expected money at some abstract point, or a place where someone said that money used to be. We enter universities because of areas that promise money but when we are finished the money has dried up. Ok let's not fool ourselves, there are companies with real opportunities to make money so, let's go there. They know exactly the type of employee that they need to hire so you will have to change a lot to get in there. I can't tell you what to be. What I will say though is know exactly why you are doing what you are doing and how it resonates with the real you. Three score and ten, not promised to everyone but a standard of years. Take sixty of those depleting your energy and after try to find purpose and see what happens. I guess we have all done it at some point, had regret. Real regret is the eternal kind, the reincarnation kind when you are working on what would be called a simple skill but you spend lives doing it. The choice is always yours.

The desire for spiritual awareness is not rooted in having your community see you in church, it is not about the pastor telling you that you are forgiven without any work or improvement. The only person that will know where you are and how much work is needed is you. Once you grow gradually in your process, you will do the work. The absence of fear and the critical observation you employ prepares you to be successful on your journey. OK, why now, why 2016? Look around and in the media, our values continually change. We are caught up in multiple power shifts and the new grab to secure the future. 2016 feel like the beginning of the rest of our lives and the world needs us now to be honest, discerning minds who are aware of what is at stake. If you don't know that the stakes are not measured in dollars but in lives then you have not been paying attention. Whether war, terrorism, Ebola, Zika, the end result is lives lost for both born and unborn victims. It's all economics. The world cannot be decided by these economic types anymore. They have already had their summit in France to decide what the future of our products are going to look like and who will control the patents. So then, how many hundreds of years will we be buying from them? We have to get a hold of ourselves so that we can use our gifts of free will and creativity to free ourselves from this monopolistic materialistic money cyclone that is gripping the world.

The danger in letting your image be moulded by the status quo is finding that you look up to someone else thinking that they are living a better existence than you. Then the line gets blurred and you don't know if it is because the person has money or fame. I don't know which is worse, that celebrities become our 'idols' that we worship or that they don't even have the experience that we think they have. The cycle is so empty. Believe in yourself and worship life in creation. That may have far reaching implications for a lot of us because we don't pay attention to trees, plants in general, insects, animals and the living planet that sustains us. If you have to worship something find it in the relationship you have with yourself within this experience. The subtlety and simultaneously complex arrangements within creation which can only really be understood in the mind. Remember the higher mind knows and is watching to see if you will work it out in the ego state because it is only then that both can work together. The reward of that would be to regain access to some of your knowledge. Don't let these network sports stars, musicians, politicians, aristocrats, business giants try to steal your focus. It is ok to love you and to build you, eventually once the time is right, you will germinate like a seed and become the system to disseminate that love. All you need are the right conditions, the right soil and a little watering and what is in you will blossom.

Creator VS God

Let me start this segment by saying that I am not an 'atheist'. The source of all this energy in creation demands the honour of being 'The Most High'. The originator of this plan will be referred to here as the 'Creator'. The mistake that we keep making is to personify the 'Creator'. This is an insult to the 'Source Mind' as it limits the possibility of the 'All'. The 'Creator' cannot be bound by ideas of gender, race, matter, morals, space and time, science, civilizations, desire, regret, attachment and all the other musings that occupy our lives. This entire creation exists because of the will of the 'Creator' and serves the purpose of the 'Creator'. Universal Law flows from the 'Creator' but these Laws cannot bind the 'Creator'. It is the awesome power of this 'Being' that brought us into knowing creation and all 'Its' other creations in creation. Other than looking at the power our focus should be shifted to the creativity and the interplay between complexity and subtlety that is employed in our Universe. This reality that we share, through perception and the creation that we share through consciousness are all gifts from the 'Source Mind'.

The examination of our environment, our body and matter yields to the conclusion that the vibration of the 'Source' may well be something unattainable in our current form. That may not be a bad place to be though because there was a time when the Hindus told us that the 'infinite could not be grasped by the finite mind'. Now we are encouraged to use our imagination to reach out in the vast cosmos and gain knowledge. The perception of the senses comes into focus here as they do not help to go beyond a certain level. The brain is always calculating and measuring and substituting information to create perception. We must find a different way of knowing to unlock a higher level of experience. Everything happens in the mind of the 'All' and it is useful to remember this when we are told that things under a microscope behave differently just because it is being watched. When we assign mind energy to observe the workings of mind energy, strange things happen. Here is the seat of 'magic', anything that we cannot control is magic for us. Certainly if we can use it while not understanding it, then we have mastered the magic.

What do we need in God? Defining the 'we' can help to identify the need. The focus can be on human beings, this round of civilization, a particular race, a particular nationality or an individual. There are those among us who are religious but have no God. Buddhist and Zen followers have no God. Indians identify as a race and a nationality and they needed a God and system that is suited to their outlook on life. The Indians are the leaders on the planet in terms of known religious and spiritual pursuits rivalled by the Tibetans who adapted a form of Buddhism with great success. When viewed in this way the need for multiple Gods should start coming into focus. In each case where a God is worshiped there is the idea that it must be a supreme authority and this, to me, causes the confusion among members of our civilization. The purpose of a God is to be known, personified and relatable. For many religions to work, the deity must be able to come to you and save you from peril. Gods can come from men, prophets can evolve into saints and men can lead systems without the need for a God. We have the example of the Buddha where no God is required, the Christ who was a man and became a God and Mohammed who came after Christ with a more specific message for a particular group of people. It seems to me that the God provided matched the need of the people targeted for a particular flavour or goal. The aim here though is to suggest that the 'Creator' should never be confused with these Gods. These Gods are limited to the confines of our imagination.

History is littered with civilizations and their Gods who are now forgotten. We don't call their names, don't pray to them and most importantly we don't expect them to come to our aid in times of peril. Those of us who take the time to appreciate the vastness of the cosmic design will appreciate that there is room enough for a God to be kept thoroughly busy. I would never deprive anyone of their God but know that there are levels above even that being. That is great news for us because now forever takes on a whole new dimension and our immortality comes into focus. Your immortality does not lie in a church. It's yours to embrace and understand how to use it. Consciousness is the great gift of the 'Creator'. Consciousness that knows itself as part of the human story is where we find ourselves. It is useful to keep reminding ourselves that matter does not exist and only consciousness and vibration are happening though we perceive worlds. The question that emerges is 'what is the quality of consciousness that the 'Creator' seeks to develop in us?' This quality presents itself as a starting point in the vastness of creation. The development of the soul seems to be through the mind as a mental/emotional quality that will put us at a level in creation. This plan has been carefully crafted in the mind of the 'ALL' for a purpose that we are not yet able to receive. The process of evolution takes on a new meaning and is critical to the 'Creator's' plan. To become a fan of the divine plan is easy and to love the intricacy of the 'Source Mind' as evidenced by its work is possible and may even be described as natural. Finding your place in creation though and using your will to choose to perform that role and bring life to the possibility of creating, congratulations, we just exercised our imagination but emotionally it fits.

DEATH

For eleven years of this incarnation I had been spared any kind of loss. Things changed suddenly in 1988 when my aunt died. She was about thirty two and left one daughter and she was the pseudo-matriarch of my mother's family after their mother migrated to work. I remember being in my school uniform at the Anglican Church in La Romaine waiting for the funeral to start. The church was on the main road so every time I visited that community after that I had to check to see if I could see the head stone as I passed by. That was a different time and they still buried people in the church yard. After that though death visited with a frequency that made me sick. The following year my uncle died of a brain tumour. My mother was really fond of her big brother. The next to go was my mother's partner of three and a half years. Strangely enough he too died of a brain tumour. It would not be long until my mother would migrate to work just like her mother. In 1990 during the curfew that followed the coup attempt in Trinidad, my great grandmother of ninety four died of pneumonia. She died in the house with us at eleven o'clock on my birthday and we had to wait until six o'clock to remove the body. Five years later my uncle came to us in tears, his children's mother was dead and he wanted to take his two children to live with him and he needed our help.

Then death took on a really sinister feel. The loss of two infants to problematic pregnancies took me for an emotional ride that made the few years that I dealt with that seem surreal. My first wife and I endured those incidents one after the other and I don't know if we ever really recovered. Then about six years ago I got the worst death news of my life. I was in a restaurant in Port of Spain having a drink with two co-workers when my phone rang. It was my uncle's wife and in a very calm voice she told me that my thirty one year old cousin and her two children were dead and that police were at the house investigating. I could not move for an hour and it took everything in me not to let on about the news that I had gotten. I got to the house about an hour and a half later and the bodies were still in the house. I watched them bring out the body of someone I had grown up with and loved like a sister. The loss of those children rocked the community. She was murdered, and who could kill children like that. Death had changed forever. Then came news of another female cousin who had gone to France to teach English. Meningitis, she lasted two day in the hospital after contracting the disease and she was declared brain dead. Just a few months before she was scheduled to return to Trinidad, she came home in a box. An uncle present at the funeral was telling me about how much I looked like him and that I could be mistaken for his son, well he was gone within a year. Complications with his liver. Just after coming back to Trinidad for my uncle's funeral, his sister was diagnosed with cancer. This particular aunt was the surrogate for my own mother who helped to raise us. It was her daughter who had been murdered. Now she fought with cancer, and after six rounds of chemo-therapy, lost to the disease less than a year after being diagnosed. My mother's mother was the last to depart this life and closed a chapter in our lives as she had set many events into motion and now, with her passing we had to look to new sources for answers.

Fear is the most common barrier to living your spiritual existence. Chief among the many fears, is the fear of 'death'. Once we exclude reincarnation we amplify the need to be attached to this life and therefore the most dreadful development is the 'end'. This fear of death is a very powerful tool in our world. We can be controlled by the threat of death and only the most extreme of circumstances can get us to go beyond this fear and actually put our life on the line. The generally accepted concept is that if we don't fear death then life will have no value. There is another way. When placed in the context of your soul contract and your intention, the decision to make the 'ultimate' sacrifice can be an important step. Your planning for generations cannot take place unless you can look beyond your own mortality and let go of possessions. This feeds back into the bloodline transference of gifts and tasks where no real progress can be made if we deal with things in only one time and space. Death can be managed to fit within a narrative. Do we set the narrative? Not completely but the free will system leaves things fluid to some extent. The importance of knowing how we identify with roles and how strongly we need the rewards of identity, will help us manage what we can manipulate in our lives, even including our death.

It has become common place in the world today for people to threaten loved ones and anything that we identify with to get control of our actions. Nothing trains us to deal with this in society. Your general outlook on life is the only thing that will help you cope with that. Preparing your awareness as a spiritual being is important to put things in context and help you stand your ground because you know what you are fighting for and that you are not alone in your battle. Your ego state is always backed by the higher mind and over soul. This is your knowledge and your experience as a soul and death and fear can never have dominion over them. The ego dies with the body but the consciousness expands, death is the return of our knowledge and all our experiences. There is no finality, only continuity. If we shed the ego willingly at different times when we are alive what is the significance of parting with it for good. It is possible to know who you are beyond the ego. To be successful it might even be advisable that you know yourself beyond your ego.

Why is death a mystery? The main reason I can see is that we exclude reincarnation and all that comes with it. Then we create these template like services to send off the departed soul. We claim that the service is for the living but the Tibetans know that the funeral has purpose for the newly departed as well. The body being shed, leaves the consciousness trying to make sense and organise its thoughts to figure out what to do next. We are told that when it drifts away from memory scenes it enters a state where the mind energy is all. Transition will depend on the consciousness freeing itself of this alternate realm energy state. While here we can create our heaven or hell based on how we see ourselves or based on our fears. It would be more useful to instruct the soul in the funeral, letting it know that it has to move on and that it is loved. Any scripture used should be specific to the person's experience and give enough time for loved ones to speak about how they feel about the passing. The funeral should not be confined to a rigid program.

Death is sometimes used to end pain and frustration. Either by turning on others with murderous intention or by turning on ourselves through suicide. Suicide is one of the greatest transgressions against the spiritual system that arranged for your presence here. Suicide as an answer is short lived as we are returned here a very short time after, under similar conditions to live out the soul contract. The amount of people who end their own life on the planet is always a large proportion of the population. We also resort to murder as a solution to our problems but this is a clear indication of our spiritual level. Lust, jealousy and hate are born of low vibration frequency. These are easy to come into contact with and with no mastery of self we are easily swayed to act in accordance with these emotions. Thoughts give rise to emotions and vice versa, so we must resist low vibration thoughts, to create a higher level vibration. When we do this we are not being saintly or pious but rather we are saving ourselves from sinking into a sea of negative vibration that is always present as an antecedent to our spiritual development. My mentor always says, "the price of freedom is eternal vigilance". We are always required to remember that each case must be evaluated on its own merit and subtlety is always a factor as life and creation are a combination of complexity to amplify subtle gems of experience. Love life though it may not seem easy and the more aware you become raises your frustration but also raises your ability to attract better information.

Death is an extension of the time and space equation in creation. Nothing can be measured without a beginning point and an end point. Death marks an end point to a specific focus during the experiment that we are a part of. An opportunity to tweak with the variables. The emotion body is powerful but understanding death in this way can help us deal with the loss without creating unnecessary karma due to pain. Who we are beyond death is always with us, but the identity state is allowed to exercise its free will in a body and deal with the consequences. We must find a better way to benefit from the lessons of death in our community. Funerals are usually community gatherings and people leave these gatherings at a level of mental activity that is higher than usual. This need not be wasted as families who fight for material gain must look at themselves during this time. People who are selfish to the detriment of others must look at themselves at such time. People who have lived their whole lives ignoring that longing inside to find the source will have stirrings at this time. Death is not the villain that it was made out to be!

The Mind

How do we know that we are alive? The brain seems to be the only thing available to us to calculate our situation. Everything is connected to the brain, it is likened to the central processing unit. The brain is organic and we know it deals with electricity. Scientists have admitted that they don't know how the brain turns electrical pulses into a picture or rather an experience. It's like this organic 'analogue to digital' convertor! The limitations of the brain are known and are linked to the limitations of the receptors. Perception is built in pieces as the environment can only be observed in pieces at a time. So we can agree that the brain is finite and limited and can possibly benefit from upgrades in several areas. Is the brain and the mind the same though? The answer to this question creates a paradox where the mind exists outside of the brain while using the brain to create an experience. This reinforces two ideas, which are that matter is not real and energy is provided by a source outside ourselves.

How do we know our mind? It seems to be this floating feeling of presence that can observe one's self while knowing other things outside of the identity of one's self. It is like nothing else that we ever experienced but we take it for granted because we use it for everything. This brings us to thought! We know our mind through thought, either because thought is born in the mind or the mind has dominion over thought energy. I can't say which, it is a mystery to me. However through this interplay of mind, thought and electrical pulses, we are aware of life. Consciousness, it would seem, uses these components to accomplish its agenda. We are told that the mind can be fractured and controlled. The description of the mind as a 'perfect cube' with sixteen compartments and an arrangement between a higher and lower mind serves to give a view to understand and defend the vulnerable aspects of the mind system. We are told that when the mind is attacked, it sacrifices the lower mind and the higher mind withdraws and protects itself from harm. We often talk about the 'subconscious' but are we willing to venture into the realm of the subconscious to reclaim what we have forgotten?

The mind is our starting point on our journey of spiritual development as we observe the natural inclination of our identity state and the kind of thoughts that come to us as we cope with our reality. Taking instruction from our higher mind is difficult at first, as the subtlety of the guidance is the first obstacle. We always have an ideal view of our behaviour, the trick is being able to see what our true actions create and the influences that drive our actions. This is not an overnight process and we should not look for overnight success. The next shocker is that this type of introspection never ends. The mastery of self-analysis must always be employed to keep the mind grounded and the intention clear. The intention does not exist by itself but rather is always linked to the emotion-body and self-image. The mind is also clever in terms of justifying behaviour and deceiving the self. The goal must be clear and the outcome measurable. Becoming a better person is a vague goal and being pious is pointless as the mind is a formidable opponent.

Progress in the area of living with the mind can manifest numerous benefits. Controlling the reactions to events, predicting developments in relationships, communicating better to spouse or partners, being more open to your children and their needs, caring more about the tools they have to succeed, spending less time worrying and more time preparing, understanding the balance between sacrifice and gain, but most importantly amplifying the power of your intention. The misconception is that being a spiritual person is the same as being a recluse. The reality for most of us though is that we have to live in our lives with this new responsibility for self and a heightened awareness of our environment, with little control over how our family and neighbours chose to act. Being a spiritual energy being means life through different dimensions as you experience fantastic unbelievable experiences in the astral state but return to very mundane application as you live and bond with others. If you are fortunate, there may be people who you can talk to and share with, but in most cases you will have to be strong and be that light to your loved ones as they burden you further while saying what a nice person you are. Loving is important in every environment but remember to love yourself too.

I have been told that I wear my heart on my sleeve and I analyse things too much. I take life too seriously and that I should lighten up and have fun more often. These were always described as personality traits but I never was able to interact with my personality. My mind on the other hand is always accessible. Fortunately for me my need to conform was not so strong that I would take drugs or depress myself because of these criticisms. As it turned out these traits that they described were more like gifts and when I started to trust myself to believe that I could figure out what was best for me, my world started to change. The cautious observation of the mental processes, focus on subtle changes in environment and reaction and the things that help us build the 'them and us' mind constructs will go a long way to instruct us on who we are and where we are in our development.

We are always alone because we experience the world in our mind. In a very real sense there is no matter so there is nothing else but mind energy. So it is amazing that a consciousness can be taught to be afraid of the idea of being alone. Many lives are ruined because people make decisions to avoid being alone sometimes as a short term fix and other times as a long term fix. We believe in this so much that in our prisons the strongest punishment that we can threaten is 'solitary confinement' for long periods. Introspection is the opposite premise where there is value in seeking out time spent with the mind to understand how we use our energy, waste time and create the world of confusion that consumes us. Here we rearrange our priorities regardless of how others feel and focus on the acts that speaks to us because we have to navigate back to our centre. The mind is powerful, the mind is subtle, the mind is complex, and the mind is simple but always remember while trying to understand your mind that all this is taking place in the mind of 'The ALL'.

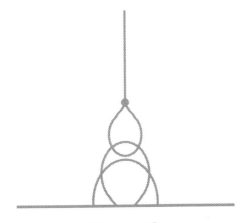

Part 2

'Be the masterpiece and the work in progress simultaneously'

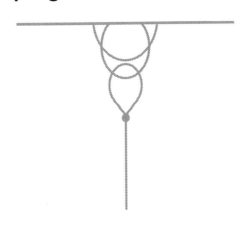

Vision

For the majority of working class people in the Caribbean, poverty is a reality. Poverty though, takes on a dark meaning when people can't cope, unable to have a clear idea of what they are working for and what comes next, when there are no mile stones of achievement and just a constant grind of drudgery. Poverty can steal your hope if you let it. This prompts my definition of vision as the ability to 'see' a path through the chaos to help define clear goals. With observation, introspection and vision we hone our ability to have laser like intention. Vision should go beyond what we receive with our eyes as we analyse events in and outside of our environment to expect change. We may not be able to work out all the details but there is a level of awareness that should be maintained. Have you ever asked yourself how much you observe? Is there more going on around you than you are aware of? It is perhaps unfair of me to ask these questions as I am trained to listen, observe non-verbal communication and pry into the nature of statements that people make. It is necessary though to develop insight into what happens within both current and possible future events. There is nothing supernatural about it, things are correlated and if we work out the ordered pairs then we should not be surprised by the reaction.

Vision here does not allude to premonition nor to precognition, it is a state of living where we collect much more of the clues that are always around us so that we can be surprised less frequently and be a little more stable emotionally. Socialization through education teaches us what is important and what is irrelevant. What we should value and what we should throw away. Vision must pander to an individual agenda and is a very personal skill. It is useful at every stage of the developmental process to know how much ground has been covered and a fair estimate of the work to come to be able to execute your intention. The spirit being experiences vision differently as it is not a question of seeing for the conscious mind but a state of feeling. Feeling connected to a situation or a project and its outcome.

It's mid-August and I have opted to leave Trinidad for a few weeks for vacation. The lure of beautiful beaches and staying at a nice resort is an international standard for relaxation. On vacation though, we have the ultimate choice, be the tourist and accept things at face value or peer behind the façade to see the real people and circumstances that resort life is built upon. Some people would say why would you spend money and then try worrying about things to spoil your experience? Ok, on this point I agree. You unplug, you relax and unwind and pretend that life is all about fun and that this place was provided for you to do that. Good! Yes it works, because you return home feeling recharged, sometimes with a fresh perspective because of the comparison of customs and lifestyle. The problem is what follows for the majority of us. What do we do with this new found energy? If the touristy place is not real and someone else's problem then when we get home shouldn't we be making a plan to fix our home space. You see others maybe in our home space thinking it's not their problem because they are tourists, so the space is waiting for us.

I love the idea of taking a vacation from my life, but is it really possible though. We live our entire lives in our heads. When we are arranging things in our lives to make sense then leaving seems to be counterproductive. I have interrupted my community projects, renovations on my house and being there for my elderly grandmother. In weighing up my decision I must have a view of all sides affected and eventually the plan is usually to prepare contingencies for as many areas as possible. This takes vision, foresight to know what is needed. 2016 poses another problem for the 'tourist', there aren't many countries left that can provide the tourist experience. Countries that I would avoid this year include USA, France, England, Japan and Venezuela. We are well into the Olympics and people are saying, avoid Brazil. We have to be informed to be able to make decisions, and international news is everywhere now. Though we can't trust everything that is reported, vigilance will help to sift through the misinformation.

There is the need here to highlight a synergy of skills to be a master of visualising an outcome. As we have mentioned, the spirit being feels connected and the receptors collect. Any project that is important to the visionary will be structured on expected events or targets but also on a philosophy, idea or feeling that will be infused in that project. The intention will remain specific as time goes by.

Precision

The ability to work on a project consistently over a period of time has always seemed incredible to me. For someone to claim that they have been doing something for thirty to forty years and more is amazing. I could not understand that kind of dedication and thought of it as powering one's will through years with a task when it was simpler. The task has to be part of who you are and the energy source does not have to be so aggressive. Earlier on in my life I was introduced to the standard that suggested that most projects could be completed in seven years. As a young man of twenty three, you can imagine how my mind would deal with the prospect of a project taking seven years to get results. Later I discovered that early estimates for completion could have ignored certain aspects of quality. We never take into consideration how the seven years would change us. So the next milestone is ten years as we take two steps back and observe with a wider perspective. Around twenty years something really interesting happens, where we start identifying ourselves by what we do. So we are the sports enthusiasts, musicians, artists, architects or writers etc. All the while you are building something through the years with a specific focus. Every point of development better than what you had before. Every breakthrough a 'masterpiece' though you know while breath fills your lungs, that this work in progress will continue.

I have been fortunate to know an extraordinary human being who has developed his craft for more than forty five years and has been a student of life for even longer. For years I observed his behaviour as strange as it deviated from the common practices that people engaged in. He was reliable, dependable and he cared when everyone else rationalised that they should be focused on their own projects. He observed what was going on with the youth and used considerable parts of his income to help families and support people with ideas. For a lot of years his efforts fell on persons who lacked the gratitude or culturing to bring any pleasant return on investment of time and energy. I am just grateful that he never changed his outlook on life because I was one of the prime beneficiaries of his grace. I always knew he had a spiritual core to him but it was not presented in the traditional sense. It was not wrapped in a robe, placed in a church requesting that I offer my attendance or reverence. Instead it was presented as an ordinary man doing more, seeing more, caring more which evoked a question in me. How can he do that when all around him says it's not necessary or labelled it as weak and stupid? I had stumbled onto something here and spent the following years understanding the source of this type of greatness. Learning as he said, 'to do as I would be done by'.

I visited an island off my vacation destination yesterday. It promised some of the best beaches in the Caribbean and pristine beauty. I had not visited for ten years. What I found were average beaches and structures constructed in places that were virgin before. What had happened to this little jewel in the Caribbean? Some would say progress. I would say time and construction without vision or precision had happened! We can be guilty of the same carnage in our lives. Always doing while not building anything in particular. I am particularly concerned with the fact that families no longer pass down skills through generations. No one has to make anything anymore, we will order everything off of 'e-bay' and if it's not there it's not worth having. The Europeans still organise things by bloodline. African tribes still organise things by bloodlines. Caribbean people though seem to still be reeling from the aftermath of slavery where we want to forget our ancestors and all that they would have taught us. The thirst to be modern and even post-modern leaving us with almost no soul, no story to tell but our credit cards and our internet purchases.

Points of convergence within information, triangulation of seemingly unrelated events, tracking truth with a single minded precision to unlock the subtle gems of experience that was always meant for us as aware beings. A journey through growth and becoming more while anchored by our past, using identity as context only. Loving yourself, loving others, loving life all within context. In this approach truth does not have to be absolute once it leads us to the next evolutionary step in our thinking. Imagine the loneliness of trying to communicate something to another mind which has no experience or desire for anything different.

Role Play

The 'identity' is based on playing a role. Each person is expected to take on several roles simultaneously to present an identity within the program of our reality. If you look at yourself you will realise that you are many things, characterised by your gender, educational background, physical ability, career, offspring, community status etc. The challenge is to make it work to some extent, to develop a kind of mastery in this complex projection of who you are. In this time a woman can be a university graduate, mother, flight attendant, wife and president of the workers association all at the same time. It may or may not work but in this time she is encouraged to try. People in general in 2016 have low tolerance for being told how to combine roles and they excel in 'doing rather than planning'. Most roles come with rules and the rules are constantly attacked by the modern psyche. Why can't we love someone of the same sex? Why can't we have careers and let someone else care for the children? Why do we have to stay in a marriage? Why must I be faithful to one person? Why continue to worship a GOD with no proof of its existence? Why shouldn't I kill another human being? Why can't I just take your stuff if I want it?

The point of looking at reality through a spiritual lens is to understand it as an experiment with constants and variables. It is quite possible that if we take on a role but augment the rules, then we will not actually get the experience intended. The goal of these experiences is subtlety that can only be had through a mix of mental and emotional triggers. The confusion in which we live, in 2016 is the perfect recipe for wasting time in an evolutionary sense. The image of the 'sankofa' comes to mind here, a swan looking backwards with an egg in its mouth, this signifies going back to collect the things that were left behind. The ancient Africans understood this, why can't we. So I am saying that the identity is necessary to pursue spiritual growth and the identity is a tool of the physical world. The rules should not be changed carelessly because you do not know what you will miss in an incarnation. The outlook is not one of a civilization of seven billion people fighting for fixed resources, it is much bigger than that, it is a matter of your evolution through experiential knowledge to attain a quality that is desired by your Creator.

If we are indeed consciousness encased in a flesh body then how can we progress if we don't accept where we are and apply ourselves in our current circumstance? We do not control much in this form, our will is the tool that we control. We cannot change the rules at the level of grand design. The decimation of all social standards without careful consideration of what we are creating is not the answer. Our world endures too much confusion, and a lot of it is our own doing and, yes there is an attainable solution. Attainable only because you rely on no one else but you to change things. Stop contributing to the non-sense, think carefully first and only create what you intend to. The individual solution that goes viral is the answer as you do not need to convince anyone, you just improve you. That's it, mission accomplished, save you and then observe. Have patience and wait to see how your altered state interacts with the environment. Live your roles to the fullest. Be the best uncle you can be, the best teacher, the best neighbour, best taxi driver and the best human being because we need you now to colour this new era as we stand at the threshold in 2016.

Stepping into your roles can only be successful if you control your emotions to some extent. Without the emotion body the potential for messy outcomes are increased tenfold. My mentor shared recently that all art is the exploration of the emotions. Perhaps the development of an artistic skill can be a way to discover some level of mastery of the emotions. Being an adult, I strongly recommend that you take the time to develop a mature outlook on life and balance your perspectives. Any areas where your experience is grossly insufficient should be known and caution taken to reflect that in your dealings. It is ok to not know, it is ok to grow in a role, and it is ok to be mentored and to mentor others.

The mental environment that we create is paramount to the way we step into our roles and how easily we step out of them. Long before this social media era we were promoting that, 'politics has a morality of its own', 'business is a cut throat competitive environment', 'the end justifies the means', 'you get the level of justice that you pay for' and 'survival of the fittest'. We have moved forward with these things as truths and now on social media we have arrived at new standards 'where everyone is entitled to their own opinion'. It is amazing that on this planet we have not achieved standards of racial equality, economic or financial equality, food stability, equal access to housing or equal opportunity for movement but we have arrived at a standard on the internet where everyone has an opinion and it is an inalienable right to have your opinion. All we have achieved is a new way to close our minds to information in an environment that is full of information. Every revolutionary leader would say, 'if the people would only wake up, then we could…..', they won't wake up because they have arranged it so that they are only interested in the narrative that is pleasing to them. Your story is ugly and therefore they will stick to their opinion.

The Creation story is one balanced on the premise of free will and roleplaying is one of the most obvious areas where choice is exercised. There is power in a role, the power to influence a life to blossom or germinate according to divine plan, whether it is clear to us or not. We play the role by applying the faith that all things work together for good and we trust the program that feeds our reality to unfold as it should. With vision and precision of focus we step into the role and allow faith to do the rest and we observe, tuned to the slightest changes that we can muster even going beyond the receptors, honing in on mastery at this level…….

Training

Growth through life is meant to be a continuous process. The mind can become distracted by seeking pleasant experiences. Training the mind might sound like the solution but the mind can only be trained with experience. We have created a loop. The process of training the mind is lengthy and must be specific. For athletes we talk about muscle memory where the act is done so many times that the shape and the elasticity of the muscle are affected and the limbs only work in a specific way. Training the mind uses experiential knowledge to gain deeper and deeper understanding about a subject matter. If we approached life in a type of training mode then we would learn much more as we progress, make fewer mistakes and have to repeat less bad experiences. There may be merit in a training mode outlook but still the progression to mastery will not be achieved. The specific points of training will be missing. Those of us who are part of a system to bring an individual through a learning curve or more specifically a developmental curve, we would be aware that we are benefiting from the experiential knowledge of those who succeeded before us.

Life has turned into one big training camp for me and though I did not know what I had signed up for, the specific focus was present to create who I am now and beyond. In an informal and formal setting I have been exposed to science and technology and social engineering of events to observe the inner workings of the environment. We would sit and look at what dogs were doing, what cats in the neighbourhood were doing and of course compare that to what humans were doing with themselves. This was normal life, school, sports, home talking about life, reading, feeding the cat, observing the gaps in the dog's return home. Not knowing that it was all training. Learning many little things at once. Now if we discuss reality we burst into a casual discourse of the science in matter and the chemistry of the atom while contemplating time and space and always taking precautions to add free will. This is who we are now as a result of how we have lived. I believe that everyone should be exposed to the basic principles of physics and chemistry. It should not be relegated to the classroom as many of us never make it to the classroom. It is only with a grasp of the basics that we can build to the points of convergence with other disciplines to start to understand what we are.

When doing physical training the mind is always concerned with how long this unpleasant feeling is going to last. It is always trying to get you to stop what you are doing. So training turns into a series of ways to trick your body to do more work while your mind is saying stop that. And eventually you stop because you reach your limit. So one day I looked at my mentor after being able to endure a little more pain and I asked if I had done well. He looked at me and he said, 'the point of training is not to boast about how much pain you can take but to prepare the body to react spontaneously'. The same is true for training the mind. For years I was amazed that we could talk for hours while building mental model upon mental model until we had cut a path through chaos to clarity. I had never done this before, how could he lead me through my mind to the most natural conclusion in the world, and he did it consistently. Now I understand that as the standard. The sharpness, the focus, the quickness that recognises points of convergence in information. To change direction by adding information but mapping everything in the mind. With laser like precision within the mind to hunt down a solution. The solution never stood a chance against us.........

After two marriages, becoming a parent and twenty years in the labour market, I can't say that I have mastered marriage, parenting or the world of work. What I can say though is that I have gained greater mastery over me, have found my centre and now I manage these identity projects better because I know who I am. I take much more from experiences than I did fifteen to twenty years ago and my mind is alert at all times. Though the work in progress continues I am aware of this milestone as I explore deeper into myself. The caution that I would share with someone on the path is to be patient with yourself. Once your seeking of truth is genuine you will progress. It's like being baked slowly in your life experiences at the right temperature and after a specific period of time, you will be ready.

Community

Heightened awareness ultimately leads to thoughts of community. The interconnected nature of matter and reality prompts the view of collective human efforts. The application of this view can be adjusted through analysis of your neighbourhood, country, region, hemisphere or the world. It is difficult to use the collective approach to change circumstances as people don't easily give themselves to causes unless there is an obvious draw to the activity. Most times there will be a community view with the frustration of not being able to organise simple activities. The truth is, just as you are trying to start something new there are others out there hoping for support as well. It is really annoying that all the big problems lead back to an individual effort to move toward a solution. So be the type of person that would give yourself to causes, support another and it is possible that your agenda can take root in an unexpected group. However, it must be a natural fit. Trust yourself to know the difference.

Vacationing on a Caribbean Island is the gold standard for tourism. Most people don't know that even Caribbean people think about this standard. I am on vacation on this beautiful island with its irregular shape and many beaches. The weather has been brilliant for the most part with blue skies, hot temperatures and bright sunlight. Every day was the perfect opportunity to submerge yourself in a body of water, it did not matter if it was the pool, ocean or the hot tub. Three weeks of swimming, eating at restaurants, night clubs and casinos and you can forget that this is all make believe. In the middle of the euphoria you realise that you don't get the full tourist experience because you are not white. Hotel staff are short with their hospitality because you are Caribbean as opposed to being European or American. One of the things that I was trying to ignore here is that it was election time. I have no issue with politics but it is usually linked to a jurisdiction. I was outside of my jurisdiction so I did not expect people to be stopping my car to give me paraphernalia to support their party.

When I allow myself to observe this community I am amazed that in 2016 they are only now working through ideas of nationalism, their population being mostly immigrants who provide cyclical labour. It is difficult to watch this territory struggle through developments that took place in the region fifty years ago. They have somehow been insulated from the wave of independence that swept through Haiti, Jamaica, Trinidad and the rest of the former commonwealth territories in the region. This territory exists with a work force that has a stake in the present but no claim on the island's future. The inner working of the government lacks structure as they pander to a colonial type model rather than a modern independent state. This view, I must admit, is because I am a Trinidadian and am accustomed to a different standard.

Comparing my home to my vacation destination does not always work out in favour of Trinidad as I have found something here that we lack. There are more nationalities mixing here than in Trinidad and they have found a way to live together that surpasses what we experience. The mature working class people would finish their work day and proceed to their communities where they would assemble and play cards, dominoes or just gather to talk. They develop a routine of community activity and young people, if disciplined enough, can learn from older heads. As a result of this they band together in times of tragedy to clear roadways and clean up their area, rebuild structures and support families. They are shocked by violent crime in their community and speak out against the senselessness of it. Sometimes they can even defuse a situation by speaking to an individual before they do something stupid. So any negative criticism of this place is countered by the fact that they still have a kind of humanity in their community living, which is much more than we do in Trinidad.

Caribbean communities are ascribed with particular characteristics because of the lack of sky scrapers and concrete structures. We are described as warm and friendly possibly because of our smaller populations and stable climate. Our smaller communities have not had to plan excessively to survive in a hostile climate and have stayed close to our agro based origins and simple manufacturing pursuits. The fact that residents of temperate climates sought refuge in the warmer climates seasonally, we have based our economies on tourism. Just like the price shocks in the oil industry, we have had shortfalls in arrivals recently. We have not come up with contingencies as we depend on only three markets for our tourism product, namely Europe, America and Canada. We have not taken advantage of the abundance of sunlight that we have and we are positioned at the tail end of all integration of new technology. As the old nationalists of fifty years ago would protest, we continue to be borrowers of technology and takers of price. The Caribbean community has failed to take control of its destiny and 2016 has seen the end of the myth that the European model would deliver us to developed status.

How long will the region take to reinvent itself after Britain's exit from the European Union?

The Olympics are now over and Usain Bolt is still the fastest man on the planet, which is great for Jamaica. However amid protests, poverty, allegations of corruption and crime and the threat of 'Zika' the Olympics was business as usual. International brands got all the publicity that they wanted, stake holders made their money while doing nothing for the communities that lived in the areas where the games were held. People displaced for the seemingly greater good but all the ills highlighted are still there. So I guess the score here is, business community wins the gold while the communities in Rio were disqualified!

Choice

Life is offered in a mix of circumstances and mastery of self is the first frontier as we try to consolidate our power in the world. The world is full of balancing forces, those that push you forward and the ones that push back. Despite our best efforts though, this world is handled by economic, financial and social systems that influence events. If we are to succeed then we must develop a way to see this hidden hand guiding events and know when the environment does not unfold naturally. We are socialised to develop in a system that has already been figured out for us as we attain different milestones, we are told that everything will be ok if we just do this exam or that job. We are trained to want specific standards and outcomes. It is not easy to break away from everything that you were taught in your childhood and the years after, but it is required if you are to have a chance to wreck the programing. See for yourself, don't blindly accept the testimony of people who know less than you experientially.

Those of us who have gifts that were passed to us through our blood lines, sometime excel in areas of skill where we stand out. We perform at levels that are labelled as unnatural and people are drawn to us who give accolades. Among the people drawn will be the enemy who knows your gift better than you do and who has a plan to harvest it for their own purpose. We only know danger when it presents itself, unfortunately we are usually required to choose long before we know that there is danger. Too many artists and sports personalities were asked to sign contracts and take oaths long before they knew their worth or what they were signing up for. The playing field is rigged and we must know how to focus, to the point where we are not forced to choose without full disclosure. Unfortunately it is not just the professionals that need to be guarded against the enemy. Once we do not know our worth within this system we can be approached to choose a path that may not serve us in the long term but seem to be in our favour in the short term.

The best way to prepare yourself long before you need to be on your guard is to manage desire and control emotions. It is important that you do not fuel your own demise by wanting something so much that you do not see the cost to be paid or worse, realise that the terms of the deal have not been disclosed. The student that seeks truth with all their being and knows itself to be a spirit being has to get to the point where they know the importance of wanting nothing. It is a part of using identity proficiently and knowing that any desire can derail progress because of the circumstances, knowing that people notice our progress and plan to capitalise on it. This is natural and offers must be weighed in accordance with our realest agenda.

What we are in creation is characterised by various applications of the free will model. The ability to choose is the privilege given to us by the creator and the possibilities are endless as a result of the design in creation. Our choice guided by our emotions and thoughts serve to propel us through our experiences. So we have intention, desire, soul contract and identity all gelling in the free will model where we exercise choice. It may seem like a lot to consider every time you exercise your ability to choose. This is why we must train these reactions into us to do them spontaneously. It must become the high level skill that allows us to choose in a way that does not derail our truest agenda.

I am always surprised when colleagues avoid certain options and choose others. More times than not they take the convenient option where they don't deliver any bad news, they appear to know the subject matter and take as little responsibility as possible. They would do this until they are forced to act in a different manner. Then the concern becomes, how this thing could have developed to this point without anyone noticing! The games we play in the workplace usually means that we are waiting for that imaginary person, who is different from us and exists in the organisation for different reasons than us, to fix the problem. We wait years for that super manager, that natural born leader with all the characteristics to make the best choices for all of us simultaneously. Leaders being born rather than being made, so we wait..............

Homecoming

Soaring over Port of Spain at night can be a treat for a returning Trini. With the right weather and a window seat, the lights on approach to Piarco International Airport is one of the most welcoming sights for any returning resident. After almost a month my desire to return home had started. The vacation had worked out better than planned but still there was this unsettled feeling inside. What draws us back to a place? What makes a place feel like home? The moment the plane touched down I started to feel better because now everything started coming back. The culture of a place infects us and after a while we need it like oxygen. I wondered about if we ever get over it but most Trinis I know who live abroad still cling to their culture in one way or the other. I enjoyed identifying as a Trinidadian in that moment and knowing that this is where I belonged. It is strange coming from a second generation 'barrel child' but my life is here and I can't really focus or find my centre in another space. I have lived through many changes in ideology from the eighties when people were running to the U.S. and Canada, then in the late nineties they started returning from Canada and now everybody seems to be interested in dual citizenship just in case. As a friend told me recently, 'everywhere has problems but these problems are the ones that we chose to deal with'.

I returned home with two suspended cards, my credit card and my debit card. Part of the reason that I was glad to be home was to address these money issues that could have left me stranded abroad without access to my money. Naturally I am told that this was my fault because I did not disclose my travel plans to various institutions. So I am being forced to comply with a policy of the international credit card company who demands every detail of my movement. How is it though that the local debit card company is demanding the same details. It's a debit card, funds deposited can be controlled and there are many other ways to address risk. I have an issue here because societies are being handled by these companies and even their employees are affected by these ills and they don't complain. My safety is now being used as a tool against me and my solitary voice is not enough to stop the ridiculousness. My excitement about returning home is curtailed by the behaviour of the financial institutions that have left me without money for at least two days after my arrival.

My home, where Government spends in excess of four hundred Billion dollars every five years with nothing substantial to show for that spending! Returning to news of consultation on crime and a proposal to remove 'Jury Trials' brings about mixed feeling. I hope they know that this alone won't fix our broken judicial system and I trust that the issue will be properly debated among the public interest groups. Re-entry was a little rough this trip but this is where we do our work, apply our knowledge and call home. I will stand my ground and invest my energy here because my soul contract guides me to the importance of that decision. Obviously these concerns are tied to the physical side of perception, the real home coming is to feel your centre within your reality. I have not been able to find back that settled feeling for both my emotions and my mind. It feels like something was changed in the basic program and I am now misaligned to the new frequency. I feel anxious, expectant and watchful as my re-entry this time challenges me to tune into ever more subtle changes in my environment.

Duty and responsibility has always been programmed into my reality being the oldest son of four boys. The maximum leader, my mother would clearly define the tasks and most times the course of action to be taken.

Within my teen years it was important that I break this cycle and start creating my own projects and charting the course to pursue my agenda. To find my way in a world of chaos and information and even more misinformation. It is imperative that we are honest with ourselves and trust in our ability to find a way through. Once we have a taste of living this life with power in our mind and heart we will not want to live without it. Finding your centre will help every time, two steps back possibly one step to the side and we change perspective, use your vision and work on your solution. I am grateful for life and the vastness of this creation does not scare me as I understand it to be home. Through the hundreds of thousands of years that we inhabit this creation and work on its hidden equations we are alive and safe within a design that was built for us to grow.

Life without fear is a great responsibility. Fear stops us, it defines boundaries and without these markers we run the real risk of doing too much too fast. Some might be worried about getting burnt out but my sole concern is missing the subtlety in design. I don't want to have to come back to pick up some knowledge that I should have gotten the first time. That is easy for me to say because we don't even know how many times I had to come back to learn the importance of that view. I would advise anyone though that they should come home to the mastery of self and enjoy the journey that comes with embracing your story.

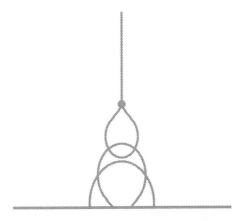

Part 3
Powering Perception

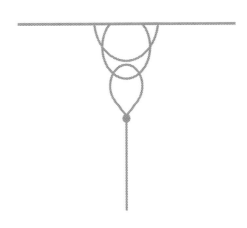

Gift

The journey is brighter when there is someone to bounce your ideas off of. For a lot of us though we traverse this life alone as others don't understand our angle of analysis or our motives to always look below the surface. The seeker needs encouragement along the way! Encouragement in the form of confirmation, points of convergence between different sources of information. For this reason I am leaving seven points here for you to use as you sift through the ocean of data to fine the truth. This worked well for me as I kept finding pieces of information in sources that seemed to be unrelated. I trust that it will serve you well.

- The brain is a digital to analogue converter and we stream information faster than any computer that we use when we build our perception. We change digital data to analogue waves while building experiences.

- The mind can be fractured so protect it from extreme conditions, especially extreme emotions.

- Civilization progresses through the use of time capsules as we leave information for our future selves. It is nice to think that you are working for future generations and providing for your children and their children but would it make a difference to you if you knew that you were actually going to return and your efforts may have a chance of reaching your future self?

- Individual progress is great but we will ultimately be judged by our collective efforts as a civilization. Hence the war in Syria is on you as the Gulf war was on us. The planet holds us responsible and it remembers.

- We have agreed that Education, as it is structured, has taken the civilization on a wrong turn as it promotes academics at the expense of empathy and compassion. We still promote the view that nature is inanimate and does not have a stake in this world. We also believe that science and technology are empirical and can only be controlled through technical/mechanical means.

- Trees have the ability to change mineral compounds into organic compounds by changing the direction of the electrons from anti-clockwise to clockwise. They are the bridge between our world and the mineral world.

- All your memories and experiences are stored by the planet in it energy record and we contribute to the experience of this living world. We should not take our contribution for granted.

The Program

The return to the topic seems natural to me as an attempt to anchor the view presented. When we isolate the consciousness, its connection to reality must be identified. The view that I present is that a steady stream of digital data is fed to the consciousness to create experiences. This steady stream of digital data will be referred to here, as 'The Program'. So in an absolute sense, we are just the interplay between consciousness and 'The Program'. Since everything happens in the mind then the energy state of consciousness meets a stream of information to create sensations. The application expanding into a world of possibility and probability. The design in creation is illustrated as the sophistication of the model comes into focus. The question arises about data streaming so fast that it can create seamless experience. Yes but that may just be the tip of the iceberg as we are still thinking in linear, limited ways.

If we postulate a world constructed in this way, then the content of the data can be general and specific to an individual and the emotions can be developed based on the meanings that we ascribe to various experiences. Whether those meanings are general or specific can be due to them being accepted 'wholesale' from the program or whether time and energy is spent refining them to carry more subtle application. Either way we are locked into the model by our emotions as they become an identifying flavour of meanings or values that emerge within an experience. The great thing about the data stream though is that it can be manipulated and subtle changes in variables can be introduced to observe outcomes. After a while we may even convince ourselves that glitches in the data don't even exist because of our emotional investment. Powerful stuff though, to agree to be part of an experiment with the variables changed independent of your awareness to see if you would detect a change and what you would do about it. Hmmmmm……..

Through this view things like co-incidence, de-ja-vu and destiny, varying levels of significance when married to varying levels of attention in our everyday lives. I advocate that we always remind ourselves that everything happens in the mind and always refocus after the reminder. This hard look at circumstances would usually yield a better perspective and allow you to have better odds at finding a way through. This is how I try to power my perception and try to increase my effectiveness in my own life. I am also grateful for the opportunity to consult with like minds. The exchange with my mentor is usually a nurturing and healing experience. Here I can share with you some of the points that he sent me and I trust that it will be received in the context that it was meant :

"We try in vain to imagine something that is everything, but, if our histories demonstrate anything, it is that we simply cannot. We absolutely need to fragment our study of existence into manageable portions, and name each portion accordingly. This necessary habit encourages us to believe in multiplicity, e.g. our inability to conceive of something being-at once- conscious, intelligent, sentient, energetic, imaginative and substantial, segues into many areas of specialized study, often leading to multiple perspectives.

It has served others & myself well, to avoid accepting bothersome things as capable of being ignored. Pursue anything until it gives up its secret or its value.

'That we learn' has taken up more of our attention than 'how we learn'. In examining, our honest options are, (1) It is unending, (2) Existence is complete, nothing new under the sun, and yet the ways in which "what already exists" can be combined is limitless, (3) Learning is not possible; we are merely remembering what was forgotten/hidden. Arguments come and arguments go, but we reach the unavoidable point where information/ data, opinion, belief and experience have done all they can to help us know, and yet, there is that "undefinable thing" in us that has to say "yes", before we accept anything as being true, being real, being factual and embraced sans reservation. This undefinable thing should be identified.

Our scientists, using range-extenders, e.g. microscopes, telescopes, parabolic microphones etc. are able to tell us things about our world that escape our limited receptors- eyes, ears, noses, palates, feel-sensors, and using various ancillary tools and formulae, have convinced us -within our range of perception (i.e. Using our receptors) - that those things are true and believable and can be used to understand/manipulate the world. While this has been going on, there has always been small, isolated groups of people, living in extremely controlled environments, who sought to extend the range of "consciousness", finding much that is valuable. Before, these people and scientists seem to be at loggerheads, but recent developments seem to suggest, that the pathways are converging."

Always remember: "A man convinced against his will, is of the same opinion."

Milestone

It's mid-September, and I woke up today after completing forty years on this planet. I feel very grateful for life, health, strength and purpose. This moment is associated with happiness as I reflect on a life with many twists and turns that could have delivered me to various possibilities but instead I am here. The love of my family, support of friends and wealth of experience presents me with an opportunity to make deliberate steps in my life. The roles that I play bring me great joy, whether its father, son, lover, husband, mentor, friend, brother or cousin. They all flavour my experience and I am better for having played them. I have not been a youth for years now and yet I am not an elder. Caught in the nether world between gay abandon and wisdom, I am in what they call my prime. I need to remember this stuff as age is in your mind-set so it too is a kind of role that we play. I look forward to playing out this middle aged role and I hope to 'gracefully surrender the things of youth' according to the desiderata. I thank you for being able to celebrate this birthday with me and being able to seal these happy feelings in this time capsule.

The opportunity to look at my boy today is the greatest gift. Seeing him healthy and strong as he wishes me happy birthday. I imagine that he is the best part of me reinvested in to the world, refined somehow. The opportunity to love him gives me the perspective to learn about the duty in love, to plan for and provide for someone and invest emotion into their successes and failures. This strange type of oneness where events in another's life could affect you profoundly. Son if you are reading this I want you to know that daddy loves you with everything in him. You asked me this morning how old I was and I told you forty and you gave me a round of applause and the post card on the table with our picture on it. You made my day and you heal my life with every new day that I get to be responsible for you. Your soul contract is written but it enhances mine.

2016, the year I turn forty, a beginning of sorts as the energies of reality arrange themselves differently to set up the next push through time and space. I am committed to use my consciousness to do the seemingly impossible, to get individuals to do the work necessary to free themselves spiritually. I keep saying that it is an individual process but there must be encouragement and signs of growth on the path. If only we would manage out fear then we could travel a bit and reap the rewards. At forty I am freer than I have ever been and still I have very far to go as the universal formula is designed to give you as much experience as you can demand. Be careful though because the prize is not to amass random experience but to solve the equations and find the subtlety. Grand movements won't do, give yourself small sample rates and sift through those experiences to find the hidden meanings. All this means is to live carefully, make sure steps and don't waste your thoughts.

As I look back on a wonderful day and a life less ordinary I am grateful for help and guidance that map our steps. Various applications of the free will arrangement applies however the soul contract still sets the stage as we get help along the way. I am a firm believer in the promise that tells us that if we 'seek then we will find'. So today I doubled my efforts to work on my diet, exercise routine and mental control. Healthy mind and healthy body is a good place to start as I journey on into the unknown.

The dialogue

Congratulations!! Now that we have established the basics in terms of the ideas shared so far, we are now ready to have the illusive 'dialogue'. For me, this work is an introduction to a more in-depth sharing where we seek a meeting of the minds, even if our concepts are not fully synced, there is the commitment to engage until a subtle truth is distilled. At that point that truth is yours, both of you walk away with something that you never had before, a position that was not given but one that you helped build and therefore know experientially. Truth does not have to be absolute to be useful however, it must have universal application. The inner working of societies, and by extension Civilization, depends on the kind of communication that we use to get things done. Over the last two decades we have seen an increase in technology but a deterioration in terms of how we speak to each other.

How many of us live extremely lonely lives? Not because they are necessarily alone but because most modern cultures don't value lengthy interacting and tackling compound issues in a casual setting. As a result, we can spend months, sometimes years between any quality interactions where the mind is stimulated. So what a wonderful world where everyone is entitled to their opinion and no one is willing to speak about religion and politics in general settings. Our young people don't spend time learning from the elderly and embracing a historic appreciation of who they are. We cannot continue like this! The model becomes truly complex as we are responsible for our education and knowledge-based application of our skills while not hoarding information but engaging in meaningful social interactions.

I cannot claim that my early life has prepared me for this type of expansionist view of open communication. My childhood was characterized by a lack of planning and limited resources. The only consolation being that most of the families on the island in the 1980s were like that. I realise now that I was fortunate to have my mother and father in my family unit, unfortunately all the interaction that I remember between them was aggressive and confrontational. I did learn though, to care for my siblings as my mother arranged this regimented hierarchy in which I was the first and deemed responsible for my three brothers. It is interesting though that my relationship with my siblings suffered because of the role I played in their upbringing as the net experiences are negative. The level of dialogue that I share with my mother, father and three siblings cannot be described as meaningful or deep up to this present day. I do think though, that we have all searched for that connection with other people to make up for the loss over the years. We never agreed on basic ideas, never built relationships, were always reacting, never planning and as a family, I would say that we failed in the face of the challenges that life exposed us to.

With this glimpse into the past I hope that you can appreciate that the current position of my calling for a better quality dialogue is a worked- on stance. I believe that with the right combination of honesty, openness, observation, weighted speech and commitment, we can save our communities one conversation at a time. First though we have to save ourselves, our siblings, our families, our communities and possibly our countries. Grand goals, I know, however at this time all I am asking you to do is review the way you speak to people and the level of meaningful content shared at present. If you are unhappy with the level, I am saying that it is within your power to influence that. We have gotten so used to this competitive-type living that we assume the worst about someone before we even meet them. Holding on to information has become the standard form in the eternal game of spy vs spy. I am tired of that, aren't you?

Paying attention to thoughts and intention and training yourself to be aware of those times when you close yourself off from the world can take you a long way to transforming your perception. People talk about taking advantage of opportunity or letting it pass you by, but I would like to suggest that opportunities may be created by the way we interact with our environment through both verbal and non-verbal communication. Learning to control non-verbal communication may be a course within itself but we must get the spoken word and our emotions under control. How difficult it is today to make a statement without people taking offence to interpretations that are not rooted in the original statement. We do not listen and we are quick to speak therefore our voices must be louder than the other person and we get skilled at cutting people off mid-sentence. What are we doing, this is ugly and non-productive!

Powering your perception for success must mean finding a way through. A way to listen and be heard, see opportunities and have the confidence to pursue the possibility of progress in your given field. To cultivate the spirit of community while simultaneously working on self, to become multifaceted in outlook and experience. To learn what it is like to be truly human, embracing all your gifts and pushing the race forward by making yourself better than you were before. Reminding yourself everyday what your true essence is, helps to keep your focus to use energy in a manner that raises vibration. It is imperative that we hold the higher vibration in our hearts and we really allow ourselves to love in a true sense. So let us start by talking, just relax and share a story about yourself with someone, reflect on the joy or the pain and observe the response. There is always something to learn from the response, we find knowledge in some of the strangest places.

Power of Prayer

The elders would usually scold us by saying, 'is this how you start your day, did you say your prayers this morning'. The idea that you get down on your knees and give a few minutes to the reverence of your God is good I guess but when I think about it another angle became visible. We dedicate approximately four hours a week to church services and a few minutes each mourning to prayers so that we do not have to think about this stuff for the rest of the time that we are active for the week. Now whatever prayer does for you, it seems like a burden or responsibility that you have been raised with. Don't get me wrong, I am not against prayers! But like so many things in our lives we need to know how to use it. If prayer focuses our thoughts and signals our intention then our request for guidance or information is a preamble to some kind of action. However this is not what happens, we pray and leave it up to a deity to do the heavy lifting, leaving us free to reap the benefit.

The seeker does not use a system that is detached from their involvement, the minority of the day is not relegated to divinity while the rest of the day is some kind of carnal gymnastics in the material world that is cut off from higher knowledge and wisdom. The seeker develops a living meditation where every day is a continuation of the last using the highest development of its information and skill to live life. After living this way for over twenty years I can say that it is strange at times, tough sometimes but ultimately rewarding. The seeker always feels open to information, knowledge and opportunity. Focusing your thoughts through your intention and doing the work necessary to explore your options feels charged with an energy from source. All things work together for our experiential knowledge but we cannot switch off because the processing of events must take place in our mind. Remember, we are dealing with subtlety, so if an experience can be had many times without us learning the critical lesson then, we should never use a casual approach to learning in life.

So we are born into this world which presents a narrative that we will grow in until we are old enough to start influencing the narrative. If we are fortunate enough to get to the point where we control the narrative then to make the next step, we will realise that we need information from outside of our immediate deliberations to be sure that we want to change our perception. We need to know that what we are changing to is better or at least workable before we make the change. Unfortunately the system most times will not provide such comfort. A leap of faith is required. Naturally, you would calculate to the point of the limit of your knowledge and signal your intention to your higher self and ask for guidance. Here, prayer is used more effectively and it does not require that a deity lift a finger to help you in your local circumstance.

I am reminded that the things that we expect from others to control our behaviour is this pointless game. We need our parents to police us, then our teachers, then possibly our spouse so that we don't do the horrible things that we know, lacks merit or value. The power has always been in us to stop ourselves, we never needed a reason to do good or an excuse to do bad. All we ever had to do was choose, at the time of the choosing the choice is always simple but the part we don't see and control is the exponential ripple in the system that comes after the choice. And it too is subtle.

We have become addicted to the idea of having private thoughts, and all deception on the planet is derived from the hope that thoughts can remain private. If we had full disclosure on this planet then a lot of the confusion would be removed. I mentioned this point to say that the same sickness has crept into prayer. Some of us believe that the communication that we attempt while praying is for the deity because only we know our thoughts, and by letting them in on these thoughts then they will serve you better. So a God being there to serve you, doesn't that imply somehow that you are an even higher God, but I digress. So God does not know what you need and you have to tell 'It'. That must be why the world is in such a mess, it's a communication problem! Unfortunately, I don't think this is the problem, I am suggesting that the deity is waiting for you to do the work. If you do not make progress it is on you. I suggest to you eternal vigilance, maintaining a living meditation every day and using the information in this physical model to the limit of your ability then opening up yourself for spiritual help. Excelling in the matters of your soul contract brings you tremendous gain however, excelling in spiritual matters brings human kind tremendous gain. We are all waiting on you while you are waiting on us.........

I feel the power and the passion every day of living my meditation, exploring what I am, who I am, where I have been and where I am going in the cosmos. There is no option to feeling empowered when you know that you are immortal and there is a creation that was created just for you to exist in it. It does not matter how many other creatures or consciousnesses share this creation, what is important is that you have a mission to figure it all out but you cannot stop working. As complex as the design is, it requires your movement, in a way we owe that to our CREATOR, we must keep working and moving forward.

Lessons of 2016

After two years of campaigning, Donald Trump is now the President of The United States. The world has been observing the course of this election and though one party would claim victory, the reality is that the whole process may have registered a loss. It is difficult to walk away from this process without feeling that the bar has been lowered considerably in western politics. How can we criticise Central and South American or even Caribbean political leaders after that poor display in the most influential territory in the western hemisphere. We have all lost! Amid shifts in the power base of the world financial system with the presence of BRIC and countries challenging the status quo, this year feels like we need very deliberate skills to manoeuvre a turbulent future. While we plan the end of our reliance on fossil fuel we continue with the nonsense of allowing the 1% to share up the patents for new alternate energy products in France earlier this year.

Being a citizen of the world, it is my responsibility to pay attention to the big picture. This year we have begun talking about the wrong turn that the world education system has taken and the value of the things that we leave out of Education. The prospect of war has solidified itself this year and now in our consciousness we are conditioned to expect a war soon. What is that about? War is unpleasant enough, now we must live in anticipation of it. Who is harvesting this fear that is being cultivated? Upon examination we see that war is being used to recycle massive tracts of real estate with human lives being exchanged in the process. In our time someone must speak about these things as they have happened before but we have been taught to be silent while the influential exercise their right to execute their agendas. Well nothing can trump your right to individual 'free will' and though they try to steal it and pervert it, the elites will never be free of it as the job of controlling the masses will always challenge them.

We have relied on the knowledge embedded in our education system, like what we were told about trading blocs being the answer to the world's trading problems. Now in 2016, BREXIT put an end to all that nonsense and we are asked to press on without asking the pertinent questions and pretending that we did not see the 'sleight of hand' movement. Even our reliance on science is embedded in our education system and while things get unhinged on the planet in political, financial and technological areas, 2016 has been full of all these new discoveries in space. I am not saying that they are not real, or that we should not be told, I am concerned about the timing as space has always been interesting, it has always been there and I don't trust them enough to believe that any of those things were discovered this year. It is time that we take responsibility for our individual education and exercise discernment in terms of what we act on and guard as facts. We have been under attack mentally for a very long time, the difference in this time is knowing that you are fighting for your life, your children's lives, your bloodline and for humanity.

It feels like technology is dragging us forward through time with no new sense of self. We lose ourselves in social media and the pool of opinions that exist out there. There is no reason for people to even care about their opinions anymore. Used to be that your opinion had to align itself with some kind of fact, but not anymore. Now it is ok to just have an opinion, put it out there and no one must challenge it or you. The joke is, that by doing this you are changing the 'norms and mores' which contribute to the values in your societies. The basic building blocks of society, which you can add to but never take away from. It grows to become more than the sum of its parts and then you are screwed. So if we complain that life has no value in this time, remember we are doing this to ourselves. I would have hoped that by now we need to return to 'first principles', and not push further down this road talking about 'international best practice', bench marking ourselves against failure while denying that we have lost our way. I do not need a religion to tell me that we have lost our way. We can figure it out for ourselves, however it will take a human being that is switched on and active. Get ACTIVATED...........

Accomplishment

The beginning of each incarnation is characterised by a dependant state and each and every time we must claw ourselves up through ignorance to return to aspects of our knowledge. Knowing where you are and what you have done becomes important as we attempt to find meaning or rather, to apply meanings to events. The relative branding of your actions as good and bad is a different story but just knowing that you have arrived at a particular level eludes us sometimes. The mile stones on our journey are pivotal and though we are trained to think that certain developments are 'normal' and expected, it is useful to observe everything in context while trying to figure out the soul contract. Human beings are driven by emotions and it is interesting to observe that we can be governed down emotionally just by leading us to believe that an event is commonplace and does not require any fanfare. Becoming stronger in key areas happens across a wide range of environments. In this way we are not different, being socialised through certain growth curves based on the needs of our environment but not our own needs. Until our needs manifest themselves, we plug in to general programs and learn varied skills.

Gratitude, in my life is achieved through an understanding of who I have become and appreciating the things that I can now do. From an early age, being aware of my parents and how unhappy they were, guided me to do more than the normal child to fix things in my environment, I was always involved and switched on. This can be a trap and breaking free of that trap was my first major accomplishment in my late teens. Then finishing school; building a social scene for myself; starting relationships with women; getting married; running a household efficiently on a small salary; changing my market value by switching jobs; becoming a father; representing workers; returning to academics; setting up the lifestyle based on information that you arrived at; seeking and finding truth; living with truth; cultivating love in a life beyond the romantic notion. Looking back I see these as my major accomplishments and notice that most have nothing to do with wealth or prosperity. Wealth is fine I guess but even the rich have the problems that we do.

Throughout this work I have attempted to start with one word and let it germinate in the mind to create the models for discussion. Thus utilising a system for enquiry and reminding us that words have power. We act as though the accomplishment brings the value when we know that value is added at every step of the process. Remembering that there is value lurking around even though the process is not over, can be used to our benefit. Once it is used to improve relationships and appreciate work, then we win. Therefore we press forward one step at a time sampling the data stream regularly while being cognisant of incremental value points, to me this is how we are truly alive, switched on. This view shows us the work in living and though rewarding, there is no break. Stamina becomes a tool paired with your intellect, yearning for knowledge and keen observation. It is imperative that you develop in all these areas to start making real progress on the way. I wish the list was exhaustive, but sorry it is not!

It is interesting that as a civilization we don't build consistently for any considerable period through linear time. Three thousand years ago the planet was very different in terms of technology. Is technology the 'achievement' though? There are numerous sources now that highlight earlier man with significantly efficient technical methods, however their civilization did not survive. It is useful from time to time to take the micro and then the macro views of the challenges we face. I know you would agree that achieving anything at the level of the civilization is difficult and may be relegated to the realm of luck. The individual level then becomes the area for strategy and execution. Mastery of self, training mind and body to exercise your focus. In so doing we create, change, adapt, evolve and give ourselves the chance to contribute. Marginal differences in philosophy can yield dividends as we shift from asking 'what is the meaning of life?' to asking 'what can I do to add meaning to life?'......

Printed in the United States
By Bookmasters